A TRUE GOLF STORY...
JUST LOADED WITH LIES

A TRUE GOLF STORY...
JUST LOADED WITH LIES

by

Fred Fischer

Illustrations by John Crawford

A Geneva Book

Carlton Press, Inc.   **New York, N.Y.**

Illustrations by John Crawford

FOREWORD

The story you are about to read is true. Only the names have been changed...to protect the life of the author!

What I say herein to and about my two golf companions is not true, but it is true that I said those things to and about them anyway.

Each lie, as it was told, seemed to "string" them and reinforce itself. Moreover, each lie seemed literally to beg for another one...and, an even bigger one when possible. At the end *George* continued to embrace and believe all the lies; but, he was steadfast in his refusal to accept the truth.

Then there was the matter of fair play. After a while my conscience would not permit me to tell *George* a lie about *Shank* without telling *Shank* a somewhat equal lie about *George*. (Liars have scruples, principles and ethics, too, you know).

In the past I had always maintained that if and when I said something so utterly absurd and so totally ridiculous as to be universally unbelievable then it was not really a lie...it was merely joking or kidding. Now I am not so sure.

Shank, by the way, holds an MBA from a prestigious university and is currently vice president of marketing at a successful national corporation. He maintains an office and makes his home in the San Francisco "Bay area." And, he hits the ball much better than his handicap suggests.

A TRUE GOLF STORY...
JUST LOADED WITH LIES

A TRUE GOLF STORY...

JUST LOADED WITH LIES

(And That, Friends, Is A Fact)

My friend whose real name is _____ will be referred to herein simply as *Shank,* primarily—if not wholly and solely—to protect the privacy of his family and former friends. Frankly. I do not care a whit about his current friends. In fact, I would name everyone (or anyone) of them if only I could.

Shank will most likely be displeased with the "alias" I have chosen for him here. If so, I am sorry. But, it was the very first to come to mind and thereafter it was the only one that would come to mind. There is nothing personal about it, it is only a name. If Shank chooses to consider it an adjective or a verb that's his problem. I use it here, capitalized, as a proper name.

Shank and I flew into New Orleans from San Francisco late one Sunday evening. We rented a big car, primarily for the convenience of our golf clothes and clubs, which we just "happened" to have just in case we "happened" to need them.

After spending the night in New Orleans we completed our business there and moved on to and through Gulfport, Biloxi, Pascagoula, Mobile and Pensacola, completing all of our business at each place. By Wednesday night there was absolutely no doubt in either of our minds that we had made quite substantial gains against the clock and the calendar. We had easily and quite literally "earned" two free days (plus, according to Shank, at least one-half of Saturday).

Shank wanted to play Tiger Point, Indian Bayou, Blue Water Bay, Sandestin and the Legend Course at Bay Point. He was not due home on the west coast until Sunday evening anyway, and his wife just "happened" to be in Europe.

My wife just "happened" to be in Dothan, Alabama (which "happens" to be my home) and also "happens" to be only 75 miles north of Bay Point. When I phoned home my wife said: "Oh darling, oh gorgeous, oh magnificent one...you know that I am at the very peak of my happiness when you are doing exactly as you damn well please...if you wish to play golf through Saturday please, oh, please, precious one, do it for my sake, too. You owe it to me to make yourself happy because when you're happy then I am in sheer ecstasy," etc., etc. *ad delirium*.

But I felt that I was spoiling my wife by doing as I pleased, so I decided to discipline her by coming home Friday night. So Shank and I struck a compromise. We agreed to play Tiger Point and Indian Bayou on Thursday, Bay Point's Legend and Olympia Spa on Friday, and Dothan Country Club early Saturday. We "did" the first three and arrived at Olympia Spa at about 2:30 P.M., plenty of time for eighteen.

Somewhat surprisingly we were both rested and relaxed. We had enjoyed a leisurely light lunch before leaving Panama City. All telephone calls had been made and we were on hold for the rest of the day. The course was not crowded, the temperature and sun were reasonable (for June) and the course appeared in great shape. What time for golf! We could hardly wait.

When we arrived at the first tee, however, I was immediately seized by a severe "sinking spell." Two couples were on the tee, all in a very frisky, party-type mood. Three wore jeans or cut-offs with running shoes, no gloves and rental clubs. The other, a lady, was dressed "to the nines"—color coordinated to the ultimate—i.e., shoes, hat, skirt, blouse, socks, bag, and even balls and tees. She was giving instructions to the other three, all of whom were giving pointers right back to her and to each other at the same time.

After the ladies had each whiffed a few times, one of the men teed up a range ball, told the others to tee 'em up, and declared that all would hit together on the count of three. There was no one on the green and we had no idea as to just when anybody was last there.

Another gentleman was standing just off the tee. He was well dressed and equipped, the type you could look at and know instantly that you would take as your partner in a shoot-out. Merely as a precaution I asked him if he was playing with the group on the tee. He looked at me rather strangely and simply said "no." We chatted briefly and I learned that he had played very little the past two years and so was probably playing "up to about a five."

At this point one ball was on the ladies' tee and the other three players had yet to connect. I told the group that the gentleman here was a very good golfer, playing alone, and suggested that they allow him to go on through (assuring them that after that hole they would not see him again). I also suggested that the ladies play from red tees.

The "color coordinated lady" told me that they were sorry the gentleman was "just playing with himself," but that it wasn't their fault. He would have to wait his turn as they did. She added: "He may not know it but he's lucky. He only has to wait on the four of us. We waited on eight!" (The last four of whom were probably on number 5 by now). She then informed me that red tees were "tacky" and that she had "no intention of putting her balls on them."

Number 10 parallels number 1 and I could see that nobody was on or close to number 9 green so I suggested to Shank that our only chance was to go off number 10. I invited the other gentleman—George—to go off first and not worry about us. But, he refused...said that he would only go off number 10 if he joined us or played behind us. I pointed out that he was at the tee before we were and that it was only fair that he go ahead of us. I also told him that we would surely slow him down, ruin his game and probably even "mess him up forever."

The more George insisted the more I resisted, protested, and discouraged him. Finally, there was no other reasonable choice. We agreed to play together. But, not before I gave George one more solemn warning coupled with a very "heavy" advance apology. (By the way, my handicap was 12, Shank's 18 and I had a gut feeling that George was either scratch or minus, none of which really mattered of course).

George hit first. His swing was so smooth, fluid, and seemingly effortless that had it been an uppercut you would not have thought that you even needed to blink. Yet the ball was out there about 280-290 yards, 38½ inches to the right of the exact center of the fairway. Perfect placement.

Before my friend Shank teed up he said to me, "You were too hard on him. *I know* that you were at least partly joking *but he didn't.* I'm sure that he mistook your apparent firmness and kidding for rudeness. I'm afraid you probably hurt his feelings and made him feel considerably less than welcome." I told Shank "not to worry." I told him that I would ride this hole with George and "make everything all right." Shank said that he would feel much better if I would do exactly that because "George seems like a really nice guy."

As we were riding down the fairway George introduced himself again, told me he was vice-president and general manager of a big automobile dealership in Illinois, Ohio, or Indiana—it, really doesn't matter, Chicago is in all of them anyway—and was en route to the Florida "Panhandle" to play at least five courses there in as many days. He then asked me what I did for a living and I told him that I was a doctor. He then asked if Shank was a doctor, too. I pretended very hard to suppress a chuckle and replied: "Hardly. He is my patient. In fact, for the past two and one half years you could safely say that he has been my primary patient though I tend to refer to him as my 'client' —and for the past year he has been my sole 'client.'"

And then George asked: "And just what kind of doctor are you?" I replied: "Well, actually, I practiced neurosurgery and psychiatry, together, for more than twenty-five years; but, for the past three and one half years, I have concentrated exclusively on my psychiatry practice, further specializing, I might add, on the more unusual or bizarre—or you might even say 'dangerous'— cases. It's all very interesting and challenging to say the least; although not nearly as renumerative as brain surgery."

By this time Shank had already hit, choosing (very wisely) to lay up to the lake. It was now my turn and

16

I cleared the lake, leaving myself a soft wedge to the green. George was perfectly positioned to go for this par five, and he did just that, hitting a beautiful four wood over the lake to the middle of the green. Shank is afraid of water—especially on the first hole—so he played his third shot super safe, to deal with as little of the lake as possible.

As we were riding to my ball George said: "Do you mind if I ask you just what you are treating Shank for? After what you told me, surely you can understand why I might have more than a passing interest."

"Certainly," I replied. "I can readily understand and appreciate your interest; but, on the other hand, you must realize, recognize, and respect the fact that it would be very unprofessional and highly unethical of me to describe in detail Shank's extremely personal problems, not only to you, but to any other nonfamily layman. You understand, I'm sure." Of course, George not only understood, he apologized profusely for his apparent intrusion and insensitivity.

"But, George, I will tell you this much. Shank has been 'on campus'—that is institutionalized—for close to six years. I now have him under the influence of some experimental drugs and medicines; but, this is his first time 'out' overnight—and I'm planning six nights out— that is away from 'the facility.' You have no idea of what this is doing to my malpractice insurance premium—it is actually costing more than my fee. Fortunately, his family is paying for it. Thus far, however, the results have been most satisfactory, and indeed most pleasantly surprising. For the first time ever, I am able to carefully observe him in a noncontrolled environment under what you might call everyday type spontaneous conditions, situations, and circumstances. We flew from San Francisco to New Orleans and spent a few days driving along the coast to Panama City and then up here to Dothan about an hour ago. A real experience, I assure you."

Shank was now just off the green putting—though he should have been chipping—for a par. I had about a twenty footer for birdie and George had about fourteen feet for an eagle. It ended up bogey, par, birdie, in that order.

On the way to the next tee I resumed the conversation. "We ate at fine restaurants, stayed in nice hotels, looked over and played some interesting courses, including three of those you plan to play, and, he is convinced, 'did some big business deals' in New Orleans, Gulfport, Mobile, and Pensacola. He has absolutely no idea that our big business deals were set up—we were playing business in much the same way that little children play house. You can never know just what a terribly big deal all of this was and is to him. Please tell him or ask him about it if and when you get a chance. And, oh, one other thing. Very important. Surely you realize now why I tried so hard to discourage you from joining us. But since we are all together now, you must try to make him feel welcome and somehow let him know how pleased and impressed you are with what all he has done and where all he has been the past few days. Try to make him feel as important and as normal as possible."

Shank was sitting in his cart impatiently waiting for us at number 11. As George walked up the slope to the long tee on this par three, Shank whispered to me: "Damn! If you two don't stop talking so much we will never finish."

I whispered back: "Dammit, I'm very sorry but I had no idea just how sensitive—hell, supersensitive. I should say—George was and is. You were right, he was deeply hurt and very much offended by what he considered the unwelcome I gave him. He felt so badly that he was planning to quit, check out and drive to Bay Point this afternoon. I feel very badly about it. But it's your turn now to let him know that he really is welcome. But don't overdo it. I have noticed that he is much more content and secure when he does most of the talking and asks the questions.

George put his ball about ten feet beyond the flag and I was about thirty feet short of the pin. Shank hit way right on very high ground. I told George to grab his putter, ride with Shank and I would drive his cart to the next tee. Shank hit an excellent shot from a bad lie over a tree to within twenty feet of the hole.

As George walked to the back of the green to line up his putt Shank walked with me to the front of the green. I said to him: "Well, what about it? Were you able to pacify George and make him feel better about joining us? I sure hope so."

Shank replied: "I don't really know. I'm not sure but I tried. But there's something strange or a bit weird about that guy. You couldn't possibly believe what a big deal he made out of our trip this week. To hear him talk about it you'd have thought we had travelled to the moon in a Piper Cub and established a banking and communication system for the entire universe. What on earth did you tell him?"

"I told him very little. Actually I said our trip was 'nothing' except for the golf and scenery. Frankly, I think that is just George's way of getting 'in' with you. He probably thinks the more he builds you up the more you will like him. He's obviously very insecure emotionally, and he noted to me that not one time did you invite him to join us. I'll ride with him on the next hole and see what goes." (Can't you just imagine a car salesman who plays scratch golf as an emotional basket case?).

As we rode down the fairway on number 12, I said: "George, you will never—never, ever, ever—know just what all you have done for Shank. He is beginning to act and feel like a new man with a new mind. I really appreciate it. I only wish the rest of my staff were here to see what you and I are witnessing. Later, if you have a chance tell him how well you think he drives the golf cart—and put it on pretty thick. One reason I'm riding with you so much is simply to let him solo in the cart. You must remember that it has been almost seven years since he has driven a vehicle of any kind. Just a few months ago I was able to pull a lot of strings—and I do mean an awful lot of strings—and get him a California driver's license, which is probably his proudest possession. Before we get through playing you must ask to see it and be properly impressed"—that will put him on cloud nine for sure. Heck, I wish you could have seen him when we signed up to play—of course, I had already 'prepped' the pro—and the pro solemnly announced that if we both intended to drive the cart he would have to see valid drivers' licenses for both of us. He explained that this was a new club rule—possibly the only one in the country—adopted recently because of a cart accident involving a fatality. This was the first time that Shank had used his new license 'officially' and, boy, was he proud."

Of course I had not told the pro anything. When we signed up to play I had absolutely no idea that we would even be playing with anyone else. And, I certainly didn't have the slightest idea that I would be involved in conversations anything like these. In fact, when I first mentioned that I was a psychiatrist and Shank (whom I then called by his real name) was my patient, I assumed that George would know instantly that I was merely joking and that would be the end of it. But, when I realized that I was being taken quite seriously it became a bit of a challenge, so I decided to just keep "knitting" until it all came unravelled, more or less of its own accord. So little did I know then.

We played out number 12 and were now on number 13 tee. George was long and straight up the middle as usual. I drew mine to the left edge of the fairway and Shank sliced to the right rough. As Shank was hitting I whispered to George: "You will never know what you have done for Shank and just how much I appreciate it.

He really likes you—*and* the experimental drugs I have him on. He's damned near a miracle compared to last week. Why don't you ride with him and help him find his ball? This will allow you to visit a little more while I head in the opposite direction."

So off they went in search of Shank's ball. Shank drove, naturally. From my vantage point I could see them talking quite animatedly. As they searched the rough I could see Shank pull out his wallet and take out what I felt sure was his driver's license. George held it for a few seconds, turning it over a few times and looking at it intently. He handed it back to Shank and patted him on the back several times. (I had previously

suggested to George that he show mild signs of affection and friendship when appropriate).

Shank played from the rough into the fairway but was still next to hit. He bunkered his third shot. I was safely on with a five iron and George was right at the flag with a seven iron. It took Shank six to get down. I parred and George missed his birdie putt about an inch. At this point George was two under. I was one over and Shank was four over par. From this hole on, however, both George and Shank became very tentative and erratic and ended up above their handicaps. I was by far the calmer of the three and shot an 85 (which is not too bad for me even under the best of circumstances).

On the long par five number 14 I chose to ride with Shank, but not before telling George that I sensed Shank getting a bit jittery and uptight. I told him that I must calm Shank down and do so quickly. I also asked him to observe Shank closely, paying particular attention to his head and body movements and when possible his facial expressions. "I especially don't want him biting his tongue." (Shank sometimes gives the appearance of biting his tongue when using his woods). "Also observe his driving habits and patterns and help me to decide whether I can continue to allow him to drive alone."

George hooked his tee shot miserably. It was his first bad drive and it went right into a jungle. Shank and I were both to the right and I was only halfway in the cart when he floorboarded it for the "flight" to his ball. He braked sharply, jumped out of the cart with his back toward George (whom I could see peeping out of the jungle) and began to gesture wildly. The "discussion" went something like this:

"You are in position to do me the biggest favor in the entire history of the universe. And all it will take is for you to keep your dumb-assed, crazy-assed, friend out of this golf cart and as far from me as possible."

"Wait a minute, Shank. What on earth has gotten into you? I can't even imagine what's gone wrong with you. You're acting like you've gone completely off the deep end."

"Me?...me!...me, off the deep end? Hell, I'll tell you who's off the deep end. It's your damned friend George who's off the deep end. I tell you, that guy is goofier than a gum drop. He's gotta be the original looney tune—or gooney loon—hell, he'd have to get a brain transplant before he could even have a lobotomy. He's fruitier than a nut cake and vice versa. I tell you he is goofy, goofy, goofy—G-O-O-F-Y—got that? Crazy, crazy—C-R-A-Z-Y—got that, too?"

"You really surprise me, Shank. I can't believe that I am hearing and seeing you carry on this way. George impresses me as being quite normal. He's very polite and certainly above average in intelligence. And, he is a darned good golfer. Tell me have you ever seen a crazy person hit a ball the way he does?"

"Yeah."

"Who?"

"Him."

"Aw, come on, Shank. That guy is not crazy and you know it. You've just got yourself all uptight about something and I just wish that I knew exactly what it was or is."

"The hell you say. Just listen to this. On the very last hole, right after he gets in my cart, he begins telling me how great I drive the golf cart. Can you believe that?"

"Well, you do drive it pretty well, come to think of it. Guess I'd just taken you for granted in that respect."

"No, no. You don't understand. This guy bragged so, about how well I drove the cart that you'd have thought I was piloting a space ship. Hell, the way he talked I should take this golf cart and open a show at Madison Square Garden or Las Vegas or somewhere. But even that's not all. You won't even believe this. He then asks me if I have a driver's license—just has

to see it—he not only fondles it—he goes absolutely ape and bananas over it—pats me on the back—man, I tell you if he ain't crazy there ain't no such thing as crazy!"

By now I could suppress it no longer. I began to laugh. When I started I couldn't stop. This irritated Shank and he said:

"I'd just like to know what you find so damned funny!"

"Well, I didn't plan to tell you, but I will. George told me a couple of holes back that it was obvious as all hell to him that you were 'not playing with a full deck.'"

"You're telling me that he thinks I'm crazy?"

"Yes."

"Well, I'll be damned! Hell, he is obviously even crazier than I thought—which was a bunch I can tell you! He should be on the funny farm for sure. That's the damndest thing I've ever heard in my entire life."

"You know, Shank, I have a psychiatrist friend who once assured me that one of the most dominant characteristics of people who are really crazy, is that they tend to recognize each other almost instantly."

"What the hell did you just say?"

"Oh, just forget it. I'll ride with George on the next hole and see for myself if anything is wrong with him. But, I tell you frankly that I think he is a nice, intelligent, fellow."

We putted out on number 14 with George getting a double bogey—bringing him up to par—and Shank also having a double bogey. I had an easy par.

After teeing off on number 15, before I got in George's cart I dropped one of his head covers by the ballwasher. Shank took off immediately. Before I even got seated George said: "What the hell was going on between you two on that last hole? Shank was flailing his hands and arms and gesturing like—excuse the word—'crazy' with his head—and you were doubled over with laughter—what the hell goes?"

"Well, you're not gonna believe it, but, Shank thinks that you are crazy—and 'crazy' is his word not mine—personally and professionally I abhor and avoid the word 'crazy'—but that's exactly what he thinks you are and very much so! That's what I was laughing about."

"You have got to be kidding. I'm not believing this...this has got to be the wildest, weirdest—damnedest thing I have ever heard or experienced. Please tell me that you're kidding."

"Sorry, I just can't bring myself to tell you that I'm kidding. That's the bad news. The good news is that Shank likes you a lot—he said that he feels he can help you. He wants you to put your clubs on his cart and ride with him from here on in."

"Damned if I intend to ride with him! And you can tell him than in no uncertain terms."

"No. I'm sorry. But, I can't take even the slightest risk of having him suspect for a moment that I am rejecting him on behalf of either or both of us. We have come too far the past few days and we still have a couple of days to go. For me to reject him now—even on your behalf—would destroy the results and effects of this entire experimental exercise. Although I had no intention of discussing the particulars of Shank's case with you, or any other layman for that matter, I am now suddenly of the opinion that your right to safety and general well-being is at least equal to Shanks's right to privacy. So I'll tell you a little about this case. You may not realize it—in fact, I'm sure you don't—but you are observing a textbook case of the very first order. I have never seen, heard or even read of anything that even compares.

"Shank has seven totally different and distinct personalities: one is very witty and entertaining; another is downright hilarious; then there is the moody, erratic and unpredictable one; the pure 'way out' fantasy type; the gloomy, pessimistic, dark, depressed; the one I call his 'space program'; *but* the one I'm here concerned with and the one that troubles his friends and family most can only be described as *sheer, uncontrolled, stark violence and terror.* So please, whatever you do, please try not to precipitate a manifestation of his violent side. I am a former Marine and served time in a rugged army outfit so I am not easily frightened, but, he scares the living hell out of me when he's on a rampage."

We putted out on number 15 and I whispered to Shank: "You know, you may be right. There is something wrong with George. I don't think that he is really crazy but something is definitely wrong. Maybe he just had something to drink or smoke but whatever it is, I think it must be wearing off a bit because I think I see signs of improvement. I'll ride the next hole with him and see how it goes."

George hit a beautiful tee shot on the par three 16th. It appeared to be going right at the pin which was on the back of the green, but we all lost it in the bright sun. As he was returning to the cart, I asked him if he did not have a cover for his driver. "Yes. I distinctly remember taking it off and putting it back on on the very last hole."

"Oh, hell, George, I'm sorry. I saw it by the ball washer on 15 tee and meant to pick it up. But Shank had already left and you seemed in such a hurry I just forgot it. Damn, I'm really sorry. I'll go back and get it for you."

George suggested that Shank and I just go ahead and hit. He would go back for his head cover and meet us on the 16 green.

Well, it just so happened that I had taken one of George's balls while he was hitting his second shot on 15, and forgot to put it back. It was a black Titleist 2.

As Shank was teeing up I tossed him George's ball and said: "Here, try this high compression ball. Tee it up a little higher than normal, use your four iron, keep your head down and just swing smooth and through the ball. I'll watch it for you."

Just as I thought (and hoped) he sailed the green and into the deep rough, out of bounds. He said: "Boy, did that sound and feel good! Where'd it go?"

"Damn, Shank, where did it go, you say? You have just hit yourself a golf shot. That thing could be in the hole. Wow, what a shot! Oh, I wish George could have seen that one. If you live to be a hundred and play twice a day you'll never hit a better one. Congratulations, partner, that one was a beauty to behold."

I hit a soft six iron and though I lost it in the sun I felt sure that I was safely on. As we were riding slowly up to the green, Shank says to me:

"You know it's funny as all hell; but, this guy George has told me that he is a big executive in the automobile business...has hundreds of salesmen, mechanics, part clerks, etc. working for him. Also told me that he has a wife and three children, went to college on a football scholarship and switched to golf in his sophomore year and on *and on*. *But* not one damned time has he asked me where I work, what I do, where I live, or whether I have a wife and children. Not a single damned thing has he asked about me!"

Of course, I had specifically asked George to tell Shank about his personal life in as much detail and with as much intimacy as he felt comfortable with. I explained to George that Shank relates closely, quickly and strongly to real personal type information. I had also strongly cautioned him against asking anything of even a remotely personal nature of Shank.

Now I told Shank that he was being too sensitive. I explained to him that I had already told George all about him and perhaps had been just a bit too immodest in doing so. "Anyway, Shank, I feel that George stands somewhat in awe of you...he could be intimidated...just relax and let him talk about himself if he likes."

George pulled up as Shank was checking the balls on the green. Shank said that the one about three feet from the cup was definitely his and that the Pinnacle 3 about 25 feet short of the pin had to be me. George walked to the heavy rough behind the green to look for "his" (a) ball. I went over to "help look." George kept telling me that he was almost positive that the ball near the pin was his.

Finally, I said: "George, if you are so damned sure that the ball by the pin is yours, go claim it. But, Shank said that it is most definitely his.... 'absolutely no doubt about it!' You could be right though. Why don't you just put a ball down at Shank's spot and putt from there? I do want to tell you something very important, however, while I have the chance.

"George, you know, I'm beginning to feel as though you have much more psychological insight and foresight than I do despite all of my education, training and experience. I mean you sharing with Shank all the personal stuff. He relates that kind of info to the life he lived before and, I strongly suspect, subconsciously, to the life he expects to someday enjoy again. Thanks, George, you're the greatest. No question about that. Please keep it up...the more personal and intimate, the more it pleases *and benefits* Shank."

We had searched the rough and talked long enough. George was prepared to go back to the tee but I suggested that he check the ball by the pin first "just in case."

Then I told him: "If it is yours please, please don't claim it. I'm afraid that Shank could get far too upset for our comfort. Just put another ball down and putt from there and I'll replace your ball later."

George very carefully spotted the ball by the cup and I putted out for my par. He then replaced the ball, lined it up with a tree and placed a marker two club heads from the ball. Shank lipped the cup and had only an inch or two for his par. George lined up his marker, placed his ball down and calmly sank his putt.

On the way to the next tee Shank said: "Don't bug me, just tell me that what I just saw was not true. What a world class weirdo! I wonder if anybody else knows that he is out of his cage. Hell, the way he plays any body could shoot par golf. The goofy bastard knocks one out of bounds, goes through his fancy ball marking routine and thinks he birdied the damned hole. By gosh, if you don't believe me by now, I'm having us both committed. Look the dumb 'sun bitch' is already on the tee fixing to hit!"

Then I told George, "I think he is beginning to calm down a bit so I'll ride this hole with you and tell you a little more about his case before you start riding with him."

"You can tell me more about his case but don't worry about me riding with him anymore. I've had about as much of that nut as I can take. But, you know what? At times he is so articulate and intelligent, in fact almost brilliant, that it's kinda scary to know that he's crazy as hell."

"You can do as you please, naturally, but my best professional advice to you is that if he invites you to ride with him, do it! I know I would. But, we can discuss that later if you like. Meanwhile, I'd just like you to know that the drugs and medication will be wearing off in about one hour and six or seven minutes and I have no idea in just what state he will come out. It will be of some comfort to you however to know that I have a dart needle in my bag with which I can put him out in less than three seconds from the time I fire—that is, assuming I am able to stand close enough not to risk a miss. Should this become necessary—and, believe me, I hope that it doesn't—I would appreciate it very much if you would help me get his straightjacket on—it's the light travelling kind so it's no real big

deal—and then we will have to put both our bags on your cart and strap Shank on the other cart. He will be in an extremely stiff or rigid mode so I think that we can just strap him upright like a bag. What do you think?" (This question was calculated to get George more involved.)

"Oh, to hell with this, I came out to enjoy a quiet round of golf and have some fun. But, this mess is about as far from fun as I hope to get. I think that I'll just quit."

"If I were you I wouldn't dare try to quit. The most that you can hope for—as I see it professionally—is not to have to ride too many holes with him. Tell you what I'm gonna do for you. I'm gonna tell Shank that you are having some serious problems—which, as you know, he already strongly suspects—but that I can ride another couple of holes with you and probably help work them out. This will at least spare you a few more holes. I promise I'll take you as far as possible. But, I must remind you of one thing—and please do not mistake my frankness for rudeness—but you insisted upon joining us. And, you should also recall that I did my very best to dissuade you—I urged you to go before us, alone. So, as you well know by now, you have created a potentially enormous problem for me and, as a result, you owe me something. You might just think about that for a while."

By now I was having almost more fun than I could bear. It never occurred to me that this hoax could go on so long. But, with every little event or dialogue it seemed to reinforce itself. They watched each other constantly but quite warily and began to talk to each other in what I considered somewhat superficial baby talk. I found it all extremely interesting and amusing.

Both George and his game now began to really come unglued. He hooked his tee shot on number 17 badly into deep, heavily wooded, rough. Shank was at least 150 yards to the right. We looked and looked for George's ball and couldn't find it. He wanted to play "it" as a lost ball but I insisted that we look a while longer. We stayed and stayed and stayed. Finally he threw a balldown and hit it safely on the green. Shank, with my clubs on his cart, was parked at my ball so I told George that I would just ride in with him. After I had hit and gotten in the cart Shank said: "Damn! I

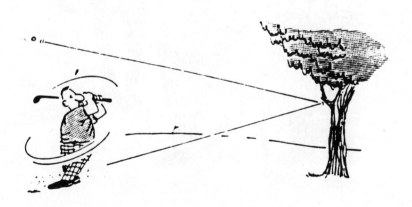

thought you two would never come out of the woods.
I thought the rules said you couldn't look more than
an hour for a lost ball. Does he just have one ball? Could
you not loan or give him one? Hell, we'll never finish
at this rate...that is assuming anybody wants to..."
blah, blah, blah.

"It may be of some interest to you to know that we
were not looking for a lost ball. The ball must have hit
a tree and I spotted it halfway there and drove right to
it." (Not true.)

"Well do you mind if I ask just why the hell you
stayed over there in the woods so damned long?"

"No, I don't mind at all. We stayed because George
was crying. He started sobbing as we were driving to-

ward his ball. And, then he just started bawling, tears were pouring down and he was shaking, sniffing, and sobbing uncontrollably. My gosh—what a scene! He couldn't stop and he didn't want you to know it or see him."

"Damned! Surely you believe me now. I told you that he was crazier than a bed bug, didn't I? For gosh sakes what on earth was he crying about? Or do you know?"

"Well, he first started crying because he felt sure that he had lost his ball—and he keeps his balls longer than you do—long enough to develop somewhat of an emotional attachment you might say to his balls—and then when we found it he cried because a tree had saved him and he could not be sure just which tree had saved him. It was a very pitiful, moving and touching experience...also very sad and heart wrenching, I might add."

"Yes, and you might also add that he is the absolute looniest of the loonies. Did I not tell you that he was and is cuckoo or did I not tell you? Golly Moses, if you do not know that he is wacky then you have almost as big a problem as he has. Wow! if I were not here actually hearing and seeing all this, I would not believe it in a million years. Damn all this fun—I'm going in. I've had it. I'm quitting. Hell, you can even keep the cart and my clubs and I'll just walk on back."

"No. I'm sorry, but you can't quit."

"What do you mean I can't quit? I've just done it. I'm through. That's it. No ifs, ors, whens, buts, howevers, maybes—nothing! It's a done deal. Hope you finish...someday!"

"You don't understand. George likes you a lot. He wants you to continue the game. And, he also wants to ride the next few holes with you. Also, he has a gun! I've checked it and it is loaded."

"What?! He has a loaded gun? Damn! This is all I need. Here I am 2,500 miles from my home and family—in the middle of nowhere—playing golf with a weirdo—and now I can't even quit because he doesn't want me to and he has a loaded gun and he thinks that I'm the crazy one!"

"Are you planning to tell your wife that a man with a loaded gun forced you to play golf?"

"Not on your life!"

"Something else just occurred to me. If you ever tell anybody about today they will surely think George is right in believing that you do not deal with a full deck."

"Yeah, I've already thought about that, dammit. Now, I'm just worried that he will go completely berserk. Why is it that when I'm with you something 'different' always seems to happen?"

"Well just remember you're the one who got us into this mess. I urged him to play by himself. And, you're the one who wanted me to make him feel welcome. So thank you very much for all you've done for me today. But, we're in this together and he seems more serene and secure with me so I'll ride a few more holes, try to calm him down and perhaps steal the gun."

We were now headed up number 18 a 428 yard par four, uphill all the way. A very difficult hole. And I was back in George's cart.

"George, I hate to tell you, but I'm becoming very apprehensive and uneasy about Shank. It's an intuitive—sorta gut—feeling, but it has proven uncannily accurate over the years. Frankly, it disturbs and unsettles me a great deal."

"Why don't we just quit when we finish number 18? I've had enough for today—in fact I feel as though I have already played 36 holes—my game has gone to hell—I'm tired and emotionally drained. Hell, I think I'll just shower and head on down to Florida this evening."

"George, I'm afraid you don't understand. At this

point you do not have the privilege of quitting. Unfortunately, neither do I. Perhaps, I can change all this in a few more holes, but for now *we* have no choice but to continue. Sorry. But, just as an extra precaution I think that I will give Shank a booster shot. I've never given him a booster with this particular drug but I'm quite confident that it is the thing to do. He won't like it a bit because it stings so bad, but I'll give it to him in the hip through his pants and you pretend not to see or know anything about it."

"Just what do you think he will do if I tell him I'm quitting after this hole?"

"It's not what I think he will do that bothers me. It is what I know he will do that scares hell out of me."

"Really, and just what is it you know that he will do?"

"Well, first he will take off his shoes and clothes because he feels that he is much stronger and fleeter of foot when he is stark naked. And, you know what? He's absolutely correct. We've tested him in a rigidly controlled environment—with shorts, running shoes and T-shirt he runs the 100 yd. dash in 11.4 seconds—naked, without shoes, he runs it in 9.8 seconds—clothed he can tear only nineteen pages of telephone directory—nude, he consistently tears 147 pages—with clothes he can run a maximum of two miles—without clothes he can run eight miles easily. Oddly, when naked, he expresses himself with animal noises and deep gutteral sounds that we have not yet been able to decipher or translate or interpret."

"What does all that have to do with me?"

"Let me put it to you this way, George. Have you ever run the 100 in less than 9.8 seconds? Have you ever wrestled a nude man with almost superhuman strength? Have you ever wrestled anyone who made only animals sounds and had no idea what was going on? Have you ever considered that all of your affairs really were in order?"

"No."

"Then we had best move quickly over to number I tee and get this show on the road."

"Let's stop and get a beer first."

"No. You ride on down to the tee with Shank and I'll pick up the beer and be right there. I don't want Shank to have one until the round is over. In fact, I much prefer that he have none at all."

I picked up four beers and headed for number 1 tee.

When I arrived George was on the tee, so this gave me a chance to speak real quickly to Shank. As I handed him two beers, I said: "Quick, pop one and start drinking it. Hide the other one. George loves beer, but he said that with the medication he is on, beer causes his arms and legs to jerk wildly and he loses all control of eye, tongue and head movement. Take your beer with you when you leave the cart."

"Great, things are getting so much better. Now, I've gotta be a full time guard for a couple of dinky-ass beers or else George will get even crazier."

As Shank was walking up to the tee George was talking to me furiosly with his lips and giving me rapid hand sign language (all obviously calculated to let me know that Shank had a beer). Of course, I pretended

not to understand.

"George your beer is in the holder and I put another for you in the towel under the dash. For heaven's sake don't let Shank get one of them."

"Too late! Shank has one now. Look, it is on the tee beside him and he was drinking it as we passed."

"Oh hell! Well, get the other one, pop it and start drinking before he gets that one too. Damned, I'm afraid we may really be in for it now. *Just be damned sure you watch him when he has his five iron in hand!*"

"I can't find the other beer."

"See if its wrapped up in a hat and towel under Shank's dash. I noticed he took his hat off. He must have stolen them while I was washing balls. Hurry and pop it before he gets back and drink as much as you possibly can before he gets back."

As Shank starts off the tee he sees George at the ball washer chugalugging the beer and begins signaling me frantically, all the while grimacing so much that he risked putting his face in permanent disarray. I motioned him to stay on the tee until I got there. I pretended not to know that George had found the beer. So I then say: "Will you please tell me what on earth is the matter with you? Until now George has not been able to convince me that you are not playing with a full deck but you are getting pretty persuasive on your own. I have never seen such facial expressions and body language in my life. What on earth is the matter with you?"

"I'll tell you what's the matter. Your goofy friend

has already polished off my other beer—that's what the matter, dammit! Now what?"

"Big deal. I'll get you another beer, but first I'd like to remind you that you were supposed to hide it.

"Don't bother to answer. Let me think.

"Okay. So now the bad news is that we will probably witness a most unusual 'combination fit-tantrum' together with who knows what all else. The good news is that he will then probably be unable to find or use his gun. And, by the way he obviously hides things much better than you because I've not been able to find the gun."

At this point I knew that I would ride number 1 with George, but I didn't want him to know it just yet. So I pretended to look in my bag for tees, new balls, etc., checked my clubs and so on. Finally George asked me to ride with him, but I told him that probably I should ride with Shank. But Shank then insisted that I ride with George. Exactly what I wanted and planned. When I got in George's cart, the first question was:

"What's this bit about the five iron?"

"Oh, hell, I shouldn't have even mentioned that. Just forget it. Try to pretend it was nothing."

"Hell no! I can't forget it now. I insist you tell me what's with the five iron."

"Okay I'll tell you very simply and quickly. When Shank gets violent on the golf course—which has only been four times—his weapon of choice has always been his five iron. No! I take that back. He did attack his brother with a seven iron once (but I think that was only because I had hidden his five). The first time I had him out it was just the two of us. He did so well that I invited his dad to come out and play a round with us. Everything was going beautifully until about the 15th—or was it the 16th hole?—oh, I forget just which one. Anyway, without the slightest warning or provocation Shank removed his clothes and attacked his father with his five iron. When it was over we took the old man to the emergency room—his head required about 200—well actually 192 to be exact—sutures and he had countless bruises, fractures, and other injuries elsewhere.

Very unsightly. But, at the hospital Shank could not have been any nicer or more attentive. As I say though, he has only attacked four times on the golf course—damn, come to think of it I've only had him out five times, this is the sixth—but it was always on number 15, 16 or 17 and we have already played those holes. Say...we never played the back nine first before. You don't think that he will mistake number 6, 7 and 8 for number 15, 16 and 17, do you?"

"Hell, I don't know. Just figure to some way for me to get outta here, will you?"

"Okay, but first I've got an even bigger problem to deal with right here and now. You see, I have to decide whether to let Shank think that you stole his beer and let you take all the risks or just give him this extra beer and share, perhaps , much greater risks. I'll ride with him on the next hole and try to determine the best course to take."

This seemed a good time to give Shank his shot as the cart was blocking George's view. I told Shank he had something on the seat of his pants that I would take off for him. Then I pinched hell out of him. He let out a howl and said; "You crazy bastard. What's gotten into you. That hurt like hell!"

I whispered to George that I had given the shot and that we would soon see the effects. I also remarked that it really tickled me when Shank called me a "crazy bastard." I asked that he think about the "enormity of that irony."

When I got in the cart with Shank I told him very

46

firmly and seriously that: "In my opinion no good can possibly come from deliberately overlooking or ignoring an outright theft. Consequently, I confronted George with the fact that you know that he is a thief but that you would have much preferred that he steal your watch or wallet than your beer. He is very remorseful. In fact, I look for him to start crying again any minute—and I sure hope you get to see him this time. But, more importantly, he now realizes what he has done—knows it cannot be reversed—and he's very much afraid of the 'spell' that will attack him within the next two hours. I promised that we would not leave him until it is over. He said it only lasts about two hours. Okay?"

Shank just very simply and quietly repeated every 'bad' word that he had ever heard in his entire life, at first singly with special repetitive emphasis on the more familiar four letter ones. Then he went through them all again—this time alphabetically, enunciating each one more clearly than I had ever heard him speak before. His profanity alphabet completed he then began to "offer" the same words in most unusual combinations and patterns occasionally interspersed with personal pronouns. It was a most linguistically creative, imaginative and innovative exercise. Shank really impressed me with this awesome demonstration of originality. And, I told him so, though I was never quite sure that he took it as the compliment intended.

Shank needed a few minutes alone to try to regroup and regain what little composure he had left. Naturally, I was able to spend these few minutes to good advantage with George. I said: "George, I would give anything if I had not revealed Shank's mental condition to you. Now that you know he almost certainly knows that you know and this significantly affects and influences both, his physical and verbal reactions and responses. Damned, I wish I hadn't told you! I'm afraid that I've done him a terrible disservice. Can you just forget it? Just pretend and act as though he is perfectly normal. It could help me a lot. And, I'd sure appreciate it!"

"Damned! Are you kidding? It wouldn't take anybody in their right mind ten minutes to know beyond all doubt that he doesn't even deal with half a deck. Hell no! I can't forget that he's crazy, even for a minute!"

"George, it may surprise you to learn that there are an awful lot of people who believe that Shank is perfectly sane and normal. Many of them feel very strongly that he is simply faking and pretending merely to avoid the trial and probable consequences."

"The trial and consequences? My gosh, man, what did he do? Tell me! Tell me. Dammit tell me now! What is he...a murderer or something?"

"Well, George, I wouldn't call him a murderer *if I were you*. And, I can't tell you anymore. I've told you too much already. I wish that you would just forget everything I told you and let's get on with helping him."

Ironically, I was now beginning to feel as though I were the most severe victim of my very own creation. This hoax had turned into a giant and it was beginning to tax and burden my imagination (which heretofore had recognized and admitted to no limits). Why had I created this monster from which there was no apparent graceful means of escape? The answer, of course, is that I never dreamed that what started out as the mildest of jokes could possibly become so self supportive and mutually reinforcing. Deep down I suppose I thought and hoped that George and Shank would both catch on about the same time and pretend that they were just playing me along. Now I was concerned that if I confessed all, both might be more than a little embarrassed at being "taken", so easily...and each helping so effectively to con the other. Then I had to think that if I shared the "game" with one of them the other would feel that he had been double-teamed and, perhaps, even humiliated.

Finally, I concluded that it would be far better for them to discover for themselves exactly what was going on around and with them (and had been for fifteen holes). My job then became even more difficult. Because, you see, in order for them to make the desired discovery, it would be necessary for me to increase and equalize the absurdities and thus arouse their discovery instincts.

The peculiar aspect of the situation as it now stood was that the more absurd my statements and intimations the more plausible they seemed to Shank and George. Suggestions and insinuations that normally would have been considered utterly ridiculous were now mere "ho-hummers." Also, I began to wonder if I had not been correct all along because both of them were really (i.e. actually) acting "a bit abnormal" to say the least.

As Shank was teeing off on Number 7 (our 16th hole), I pointed out to George that he had escaped one of the crucial danger holes but I urged him to use extreme caution. I told him to keep Shank in his sight at all times—"never let him get behind you, especially on the tee or putting green." As an extra precaution I told him that I had put Shank's five iron in his (George's) bag.

Then, while George was on the tee, I told Shank, "For Gosh sakes, don't stand in front or to the side of George when he's on the tee or putting green—he said it gives him a bad case of the creeps—always stand directly behind him." Now it was my duty to also inform Shank that George had stolen his five iron—that I had seen him with my own eyes—but to be doubly sure I checked his bag and sure enough there were two five irons—one matched his set and the other "matched your set." I told Shank that I had confronted George with this irrefutable evidence but that he denied it— "said that it was a coincidence that he had two and you had none and that one of his matched your set. George told me he was very sorry that you had lost a club but said that you would just have to learn to keep up with them better. Said that he needed both of his. But just keep cool, Shank. I'll ride with him this hole and get it back for you—he could be on the virge of pitching that fit he promised me."

Riding up the fairway I said to George: "By the way, Shank knows that you have stolen his five iron." "Hell I didn't steal his club. You put it in my bag." I said to him. "Do you really believe that?" "Yes!" "Then why don't you see if Shank will believe you? But, my professional instincts tell me you shouldn't dare try it. My advice is to just relax and let me try to get you out of this some way."

George allowed aloud that I had no difficulty at all in getting him into these torturous situations but that I always said that I would "try to get you out somehow."

"George, just put the matter of the stolen five iron on the back burner for now as we have a far more important matter to deal with—you see, Shank feels that you show him mean looks—says you avoid all eye contact with him but have a fierce facial demeanor—says you frown all the time and keep your jaws and lips too rigid. He says he does not remember a single time that you have grinned or smiled at him. And, you know what, George? He's right. I've noticed it, too. Of course, you have a perfect right to look at him using the facial contour and expression of your choice, but I can tell you this much—and this is not an opinion, it is a scientific fact—when Shank is the recipient of grins, smiles, and laughter it greatly soothes, relaxes and mellows him, physically and emotionally. We have proven clinically many times that prolonged grins and smiles actually alter certain chemical balances and reactions in his body that impact quite favorably upon the 'emotional motors' of the brain."

Shank and George were in traps on opposite sides of the green on number 8 and I told each one to be sure to let the other hit first. I then reminded Shank that once on the green he should always stand behind George and I reminded George to smile and grin as much as he could. (I assured him that one big long smile on number 8 could have the same chemical effects as would have four short grins on number 6).

Both were standing in their respective traps, each asking and insisting that the other hit first (with George doing exceedingly well with his smiles and grins). This "you go first" contest must have gone on for a full five minutes before I finally admitted that I would have to settle it by applying the distance rule. So I paced it off from the pin to George's trap and whispered: "Keep up the grins—you're doing really well—and I can just see and sense the positive effect upon Shank." I then very carefully paced off the distance to Shank. When I arrived he whispered: "I just wish that you would look at that silly bastard over there grinning. What in hell is he grinning about? 'Cause he's in the trap? Or 'cause I am?

In either case it proves that he's just as goofy as I thought. Believe it now, don't you?"

I concluded that they were equal distance so I let them stay in the trap while I attempted to determine the elevation of the traps and the depth of the trap lips to be negotiated by each. The lips I measured with my putter shaft. But to determine the respective elevations of the traps I found it necessary to take a cart and carefully view the traps in relation to the elevation of the green from every possible angle. This took at least ten minutes. All the while, I was taking copious notes and making the most elaborate and detailed calculations and computations you could ever imagine. (I was way beyond Astro-physics 802. I only hope that some day, some way, these notes end up "safely" in the hands of some Russian spy).

Finally I declared that George should hit first because his lip was higher (and his trap was lower). Shank could not resist, he said: "George's lip is higher only because he grins so damned much—and his trap is lower only because his lip is higher."

George hit a respectable sand wedge within ten feet of the cup, and while he was throwing his club aside to get the rake, Shank hit. George did not see it—and it was so far beyond the green that he did not hear it hit the ground. As I walked by to pull the flag I dropped a ball within a foot of the cup. Shank came out of the trap cursing his lousy shot...I mean, he was really letting his frustrations come out (in a rather uniquely profane manner). George looked at me with a giant question

53

mark on his face and I said: "Will you look at—and listen to—this—the man blasts out, hits the pin so softly that I just knew it was going in—it bounces back about 8 inches and he's bitching like crazy—oops strike 'crazy'—he's bitching like an old woman."

Shank is in a bit of a daze after the long delay and says: "Is that my ball by the pin?" I answered: "Well, George is over there and I'm over here, so see if you can figure it out for yourself." Shank says "that can't possibly be me right there—hell, I'm probably in the lake over there, or close to it."

I said to George, "He sometimes has great difficulty when good things happen—he probably think he's going blind. Give him a big smile or two, or a constant one."

Shank told me that George smiled so damned much that his teeth were dry—so dry that his top lip couldn't slide down over his teeth—so he guessed that he would just smile forever.

Our last hole, number 9, was coming up. Each of us had a "monkey on our back" and mine could well have been the larger monkey. I had to clear the record for their sake—but, equally important, just for my own sake. I prepared myself to confess all and take the consequences and any all other abuse they chose to deliver. I decided to concentrate this effort on George first, because I knew that I would have plenty of time for an extended apology to Shank.

This was a much more delicate, sensitive, ticklish, and unpleasant task than you can imagine. But, I was prepared and determined to summon and fully utilize

all of the tact, diplomacy, understanding, and humbleness in my entire arsenal "to make everything all right with everyone" (including myself).

As we drove up the fairway toward our tee shots I said: "George, you devil, why on earth did you string me along so long. You knew from the very beginning that I was not a doctor—certainly not a psychiatrist—and that Shank was not my patient. Why did you allow me to make such a fool of myself? And, how on earth did—or could—you keep from laughing at me for being so naive and dumb as to think you were actually believing all the ridiculous things I said? Really, you were so subtle in reversing it on me that I didn't even realize what you were doing to me. But, I admit to you that it serves me right. It hurts a bit at the moment but I can't complain. I asked for it. And, I sure as hell got it! Congratulations! big fella you have just accomplished what many have tried but very few have achieved. You have just achieved the well nigh impossible—you have really put a number on Big Fred! If I have a stocking cap in my bag, I plan to put it on, pull it over my head, let you lead me to the club house where I will buy you as many drinks as you like and give you ample opportunity to meet and get to know the real Shank...then we can play a serious round in the morning."

Now, whoever you are and wherever you are coming from, you gotta admit that this was pretty damned good. I mean it was just loaded with tact, diplomacy, understanding, sensitivity, concern, modesty, remorse, honesty, humbleness, etcetera. What more could I possibly do in the circumstances when it is impossible to correct lies retroactively?

George said: "Good try. But I'm not buying. I know a full scale looney when I see one. Convince me that Shank's okay and you've just got yourself another patient—me! See that green up there? When I hole there, check this cart in and put these clubs in the trunk of my car, I'll be the happiest man you ever saw. I'll be so full of joy, gratitude, and happiness that I may just call my wife and head home. But, I do want you to know that I really appreciate what you are doing for and with Shank—basically, I suspect that he is or once was a very nice, likable, and extremely intelligent guy. It's really a shame but I admire and respect your time, risks, and effort on his behalf."

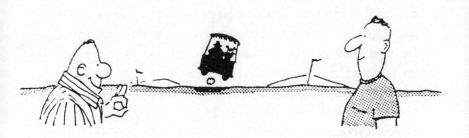

"Thanks, George, you are very kind and generous in your attitude, but I do wish that you would change your mind and join Shank and me for a drink in the club house and let me lay it all out and convince you that it was all a joke that grew beyond anything I could have dreamed of."

"You don't give up easy, do you? Well, thanks, but just forget it. I'm gone."

And, he was. As he was loading his clubs in the car, Shank walked up, en route to his room to make a couple of telephone calls, and stopped to chat. I could see it but, of course, could not hear what was being said. But, George looked nervous. It was ten 'til seven local time and two hours earlier on the west coast so Shank rushed to make his calls before 5 P.M. Pacific. He was leaving as I got there. Again I asked George to stick around for drinks and/or dinner. Again he refused. I'd had a rough, busy, day and was too tired to argue so I headed for the lounge. (These two "nuts" had worn me out.)

Shank was talking to himself as he walked over to my table. He was almost beside himself. He said: "Boy, am I glad to be away from that nut. What a basket case he was. He is crazier than the next ten craziest people in the world, *all put together*. I can't even tell you some of the pablum, drivel and crap he dumped on me—hell, you'd think I was crazy if I did. (Remember, I had urged George to share his personal life and intimacies because of the effective therapeutic value and benefit to Shank).

"No, dammit, I think I will tell you some of it. You deserve it! Hell, you've earned it! It's only fair that I share some of the most recent and profound sayings of 'chairman George'...said he 'just wanted to help'...sounded like the damned government 'just wanted to help me...' hell, I guess he could help me start a zoo...said his dog 'Gumball'—yes, 'Gumball' dammit—puts his paws over his ears when it thunders...his daughter Denise—they call her 'Denny-poo'- echos all names...for example she calls her brother 'Tom-Tom', her grandmother 'grammy-grammy', him 'da-da'—though it could be 'do-do'—pronounce it either way you like. Said his wife calls him 'monkey-belly'

58

when they are alone and she's had two glasses of wine. *But, no, Fred, you're right!* George is not crazy—he's as normal as they come! It's you that I'm worried about now...and also me!"

It was now time to tell Shank the truth.

I briefed him on just what all transpired during the afternoon. He is very quick so I talk to him in shorthand. It took him only a couple of nano-seconds to put it all together. He was very upset but insisted on seeing George...hell, he demanded it! So I went over to the phone and called George. No answer. So I then call the front desk to have him paged and/or leave a message. The lady at the front desk told me that he was right there checking out. I told her to hold him. I would be right there.

When I got to the lobby George was signing his bill. I told him that he just had to join Shank and me for a drink. I told him that I had confessed all to Shank. He said: "Did he believe you?" I replied: "Yes. Most emphatically! And now he is real anxious to see you." George said. "Just what I thought. He is, if anything, even crazier than I thought. Good luck. I'm gone. And that is final!"

I knew that he meant it—it was final. There was nothing that I could say or do to change it so I said to myself. "He's going anyway—what the hell—why not make it easier for him," so I said:

"George, have you seen Shank the past four or five minutes?"

"No, I thought you just told me that he was in the lounge."

"I was just kidding. About five minutes ago he was at your door, naked, with his five iron. I immediately went to a phone and called your room to make sure you didn't open the door. When you didn't answer, I called the desk and learned that you were here." Then I said to the desk clerk: "Lady, have you seen Shank lately?"

She said, "Shank who? What does he look like?"

I said: "He's about 5'11" or 6 feet, blond, blue eyed and naked. He has a birthmark—which he calls a birthright—just below his navel. And, he probably has a five iron in his hand."

George said: "That does it for me. I'm gone. Bye, And good luck!"

Shank and I met for a drink and I told him everything…again…again…and again! He went into a mild state of shock. Then a heavy state of shock. After he had recovered from the shocks he really got upset and extremely frustrated when I told him George was gone. Naturally—and somewhat understandably—he became slightly more upset when I told him exactly when, why, and how George had left.

By the next day, however, the humor that was fast escaping me was evidently finding its way to him. I had to tell him every single thing in minute detail. From that he reconstructed every word of every conversation in a totally new perspective and dimension. He is dying to meet and see George again. Meanwhile when he is not telling this story on himself he is insisting that I do it. As a result I have told it from Hilton Head, South Carolina to Kapaluha Bay, Hawaii and from

Acapulco, Mexico to Green Bay, Wisconsin and many places in between (usually to five or ten people or less).

The purpose of this booklet is therefore three-fold.

First, assuming that all golfers buy and read this, I will never again have to tell this story. This will please me immensely. (Otherwise, I will simply tell them to buy and read the book.)

Secondly, if all golfers buy and read this book, I cannot pull the same trick on Shank again. I have promised that I would not, but it has been very tempting at times. (Fellow golfers, please buy and read this book so as to remove this temptation from me.)

Thirdly...George...George...are you there? Forgive me? Please? Forgive me! Please! Whoever and wherever you are, believe me, it really was a joke. Please contact Shank or me (or both). And, by the way, we both need new cars. Will you take a five iron (or two) on trade?